Energy

by Arlene Block

What is energy?

You use energy all the time.
Things that can do work and cause change
have **energy.**
You use energy when you walk.
You use energy when you breathe.
You use energy while you sleep.

What has energy?
Can it do work?
Can it make something change?
Then it has energy.

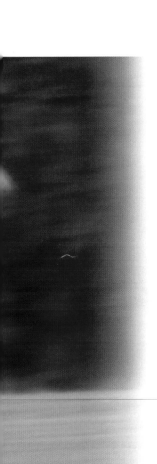

Energy from the Sun

Earth gets energy from the Sun.
The Sun gives Earth heat.
Heat and light from the Sun are
solar energy.

Light from the Sun helps people and
animals see.
Earth would be dark without the Sun.

The Sun

People can use solar energy.
Solar energy heats this home.

How do living things use energy?

Most living things need energy from the Sun.
Plants use green leaves to make food.
Plants use sunlight to make food.
Plants use water and air too.

Plants need food to live and grow.

Animals use energy to move.
Animals get energy from food.
Animals use energy to live and grow.

Some animals eat plants.
Some animals eat animals that eat plants.
The plants get energy from the Sun.

How People Get Energy

People get energy from food.
Food gives people energy to grow.
Food gives people energy to move.

Food gives you energy to play.
Food gives you energy to work.

Here are five food groups.
Eat foods from each group every day.
These foods can help you grow.
They can help you stay healthy.

Milk, yogurt, cheese

Vegetables

Bread, rice, cereal, pasta

Fruit

Meat, fish, eggs, dry beans

11

What are some sources of heat?

Sunlight is a source of heat.
A **source** is where something comes from.
Heat comes from sunlight.

Heat can come from other sources too.
Rub your hands together.
Can you feel them get warm?

Fire is a source of heat.
Wood burns to make fire.
Wood is a fuel.

Fuel is burned to make heat.
Coal is another kind of fuel.
Gas and oil are fuels too.

How Heat Moves

Heat starts at a warm place.
It moves to a cooler place.
The burner is hot.
The pan and food are cold.
Heat moves from the burner to the pan.
Then heat moves from the pan to the food.

**People use
heat to cook.**

The pan is made of metal.
Metal is a conductor.
A **conductor** lets heat move through it.

Cloth is not a good conductor.
The mitt is made of cloth.
It keeps heat from moving to your hand.

Heat does not go through the mitt to your hand.

How does light move?

Light is a kind of energy.
The Sun is one source of light.
Fire and flashlights are other sources of light.
Most light sources give off heat too.

Light moves in a straight line.
Light can move through some things.
Light **reflects** when it hits something.
It reflects when it bounces back.

This shows how light reflects.

We see mostly white light.
Many colors make up white light.
You can see the colors in a rainbow.

Dark colors take in light.
Light colors reflect light.
Wear light colors to stay cool.

Shadows

A **shadow** is made when light is blocked.
Go out in the sunlight.
Your body blocks the light.
You make a shadow.

Shadows change during the day.
Shadows change when the Sun looks high
and low in the sky.

Use a flashlight to make a shadow.
Cut a shape from paper.
Use it to block the light.

Move the shape close to the light.
Move the shape far from the light.
How does the shadow change?

What are other kinds of energy?

You use different kinds of energy.
How can you make this grocery cart move?
You can push it.
Then it will have energy of motion.

Wind is a kind of energy.
Wind energy can move the boat.

Sound is a kind of energy too.

Wind energy

Sound energy

Using Electricity Safely

Turn on a light.
Electricity makes the light work.
Electricity makes this clock work.

Do not use electricity near water.
Do not pull on cords.
Do not touch wires.
How else can you use electricity in
a safe way?

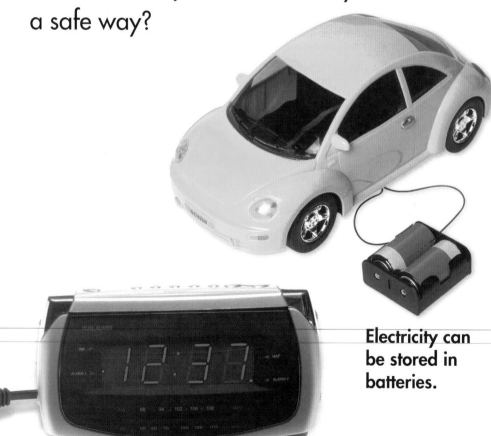

Electricity can
be stored in
batteries.

There are many kinds of energy.
How do you know what has or uses energy?
Is it doing work?
Can it change something?
Then it has energy!

Glossary

conductor   something that lets heat easily move through it

energy   anything that can do work or make a change

fuel   something that is burned to make heat

reflect   light hits something and bounces back

shadow   something made when light is blocked

solar energy   light and heat from the Sun

source   a place from which something comes